VITAMINS AND MINERALS

A TRUE BOOK

by

Joan Kalbacken

Children's Press®
A Division of Grolier Publishing

New York London Hong Kong Sydney
Danbury, Connecticut

Shelves of vitamins
and minerals

Reading Consultant
Linda Cornwell
*Learning Resource Consultant
Indiana Department
of Education*

*Author's Dedication:
To Angie Engel
for her keen interest
and proofreading ability*

Visit Children's Press on the Internet at:
http://publishing.grolier.com

Library of Congress Cataloging-in-Publication Data

Kalbacken, Joan.
   Vitamins and minerals / by Joan Kalbacken.
     p.   cm. — (A true book)
   Includes bibliographical references and index.
   Summary: Introduces the major vitamins and minerals found in various
foods, and discusses them in relation to nutrition and healthy eating.
   ISBN: 0-516-20758-X (lib. bdg.)   0-516-26387-0 (pbk.)
   1. Vitamins in human nutrition—Juvenile literature. 2. Minerals in
human nutrition—Juvenile literature. [1. Vitamins. 2. Minerals in nutrition.
3. Nutrition.] I. Title. II. Series.
QP771.K35 1998
613.2`86—DC21   97-8231
                                                    CIP
                                                    AC

Contents

Foods that contain vitamins and minerals are important for your body's growth.

Vitamins and Minerals

Vitamins and minerals are nutrients. Nutrients are the parts of food that you need to stay strong and healthy. Many of the foods you eat have vitamins and minerals that give you energy. Without vitamins and minerals you would not be able to breathe, walk, or run. You need only small amounts of vitamins and minerals. They are found in many different foods.

After you take a vitamin, it dissolves, or disappears, in your body. Some vitamins dissolve in the water inside your body. These vitamins also pass through you when you go to the bathroom.

Other vitamins do not dissolve in water. They don't pass through your body. They are stored in your body's fat. Both kinds of vitamins are important for you to have every day.

Names of Vitamins

In Latin, the word "vita" means "life."

Scientists keep working to improve vitamins so that people will be healthier.

There are many different kinds of vitamins. The scientists who discovered vitamins named them after some of the letters of the alphabet.

Examples of vitamin names are: A, B, C, D, K, and E. There are several different vitamins in the B group. So the B vitamins also have numbers as part of their names. This helps us to tell them apart. Examples of B vitamins are: B1, B2, B3, and B6.

Important Vitamins

There are many vitamins that are important for good health. If you eat a wide variety of foods, you will get enough of all of them. The most important vitamins are: A, B1, B2, B3, B6, B12, C, D, and E. People who are sick or do not eat a variety of foods

People who enjoy a variety of foods get all the vitamins they need.

may need to take vitamin pills. These extra vitamins are called supplements. Supplements add the vitamins that a person might be missing in his or her diet. People who

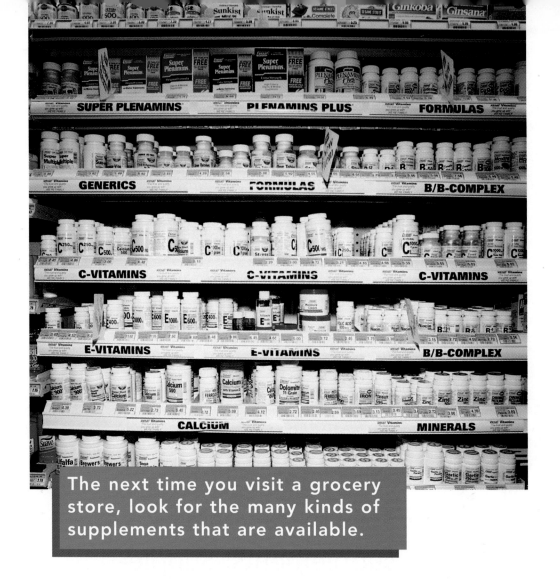

The next time you visit a grocery store, look for the many kinds of supplements that are available.

are not sure if they need a vitamin supplement should see a doctor.

Vitamin A

Vitamin A was the first vitamin to be discovered. It was called "vitamin A" because A is the first letter of the alphabet. Vitamin A contains a substance that gives carrots, sweet potatoes, and broccoli their green or orange color. You need vitamin A to help

Carrots (top left), sweet potatoes (top right), and broccoli (above) get their colors from vitamin A.

fight sicknesses and for healthy skin. It also helps to heal cuts and scrapes. Your body gets a lot of vitamin A when you eat liver, eggs,

Although your body doesn't need a lot of vitamin A, it's important for healthy skin.

Many foods contain
vitamin A, so it's easy
to get the right amount.

butter, milk, and yellow, green,
or orange vegetables and
fruits. Most people get
enough vitamin A from the
foods they eat every day.

The B Vitamins

The first B vitamin to be discovered is called vitamin B1. It is also called thiamine (THYE-uh-min). Vitamin B1 is needed for growth and to help keep your heart and muscles strong. Foods such as brown breads (wheat, oat, rye, and barley), grain cereals, beans,

There are many different types of beans (left), but they all contain vitamin B1. Nuts and brown breads or crackers (above) are also excellent sources of vitamin B1.

peas, brown rice, and nuts contain large amounts of vitamin B1.

Vitamin B2 is also called riboflavin (rye-buh-FLAY-vin). This vitamin helps the body to heal from burns, cuts, and bruises. It also helps the body to heal after an operation.

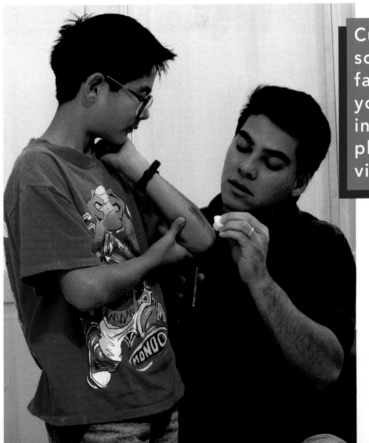

Cuts and scrapes heal faster when your diet includes plenty of vitamin B2.

Products such as those at right will list on their packaging the amount of vitamin B2 they contain. Leafy vegetables (above) are rich in vitamin B2.

Vitamin B2 even makes your eyesight better. Milk, cheese, yogurt, and eggs are foods that contain vitamin B2. Other foods that contain vitamin B2 are leafy vegetables (lettuce, spinach, and cabbage), meat, liver, and brown breads.

Vitamin B3, called niacin (NYE-uh-sin), is found in many foods. It may be the most common vitamin found in food. Poultry (chicken, turkey, duck,

So many foods, especially fish, contain vitamin B3 that supplements are rarely needed.

and goose), sunflower seeds, grain cereals, dried fruit, potatoes, and fish are only a few of the foods rich in vitamin B3.

Like the other B vitamins, vitamin B6 is important for proper growth and a healthy body. Vitamin B6 is sometimes called pyridoxine (pihr-uh-DOK-seen). Vitamin B6 is found in so many foods that most people get enough vitamin B6 in the foods they eat every day. Some of the foods

Vitamin B6 helps to keep growing bodies strong. If you eat the right foods, every meal can be a source of vitamin B6.

that contain vitamin B6 are green vegetables, liver, red meat, potatoes, corn, grain cereals, and brown breads.

Vitamin C

Vitamin C is also known as ascorbic acid (uh-SKOR-bik ASS-id). This vitamin has many jobs in your body. Some people believe that vitamin C helps to keep you from getting sick. Doctors say that taking a lot of vitamin C may not stop you from catching a cold.

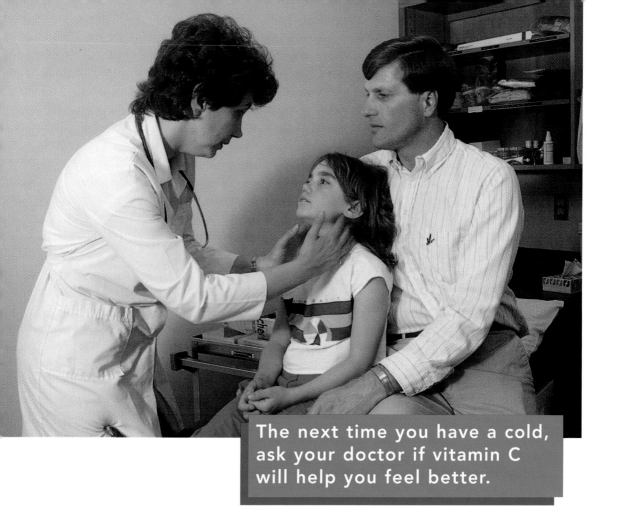

The next time you have a cold, ask your doctor if vitamin C will help you feel better.

But it does help you get over a cold quickly. Vitamin C is also good for repairing broken bones.

Some people like to get their vitamin C by drinking orange juice.

Foods that are high in vitamin C are green vegetables, strawberries, blackberries, and raspberries. Juices made from oranges, lemons, grapefruits, and tomatoes have large amounts of vitamin C.

Vitamin D

Vitamin D is a vitamin that can be made in your body with the help of the sun. There is a substance under your skin that sunshine turns into vitamin D. Your body needs vitamin D for strong bones and teeth. You don't need a lot of vitamin D to be healthy. For example, if

When you play outside on a sunny day (left), your body gets plenty of vitamin D. Even on rainy days (right), your body has enough vitamin D to keep you healthy.

you walk to school or play outside at recess, you already get enough vitamin D. If you get any extra, it stays in your body to be used on a cloudy or rainy day when you can't be out in the sun. Vitamin D is usually added to milk.

Important Minerals

Like vitamins, minerals are needed for good health and to avoid sickness. If you eat a variety of foods, you will have enough minerals to stay healthy. There are a lot of important minerals. A few of the most important ones are: calcium (KAL-see-uhm), fluorine

The minerals that food contains are as important to your body as vitamins.

(FLAWR-een), and iron (EYE-urn). Other important minerals include: magnesium (mag-NEE-zee-uhm), potassium (puh-TASS-ee-uhm), sodium (SOH-dee-uhm), and zinc (ZINGK).

The white substance that you see in chalk, ivory, and pearls is calcium. It is the mineral that makes strong bones and hard teeth. If you do not have enough calcium, your

You can hold calcium in your hand by holding a piece of chalk.

You should drink at least one glass of milk each day for strong bones and teeth.

bones don't grow properly and they get weak. The best way to get calcium is to drink milk. Other dairy products such as yogurt and cheese are also good sources of calcium.

The hard, white surface of your teeth is called enamel (i-NAM-uhl). A mineral called flourine helps your tooth enamel stay tough. Fluorine has been added to most of

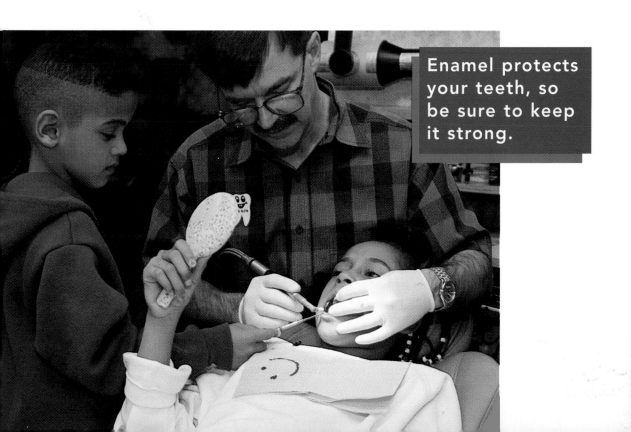

Enamel protects your teeth, so be sure to keep it strong.

The fluorine in apples is one of the reasons for the saying, "An apple a day keeps the doctor away."

the drinking water in the United States. It has helped to keep people from getting cavities. Fluorine is also found in some foods. Sardines, salmon, apples, tea, gelatin, and eggs have fluorine in them.

Oxygen is a gas that is found in the air. Humans and animals need oxygen in order to breathe. Iron is an especially important mineral. It carries the oxygen you need through your blood and into your muscles. People who feel weak and become easily tired may not have enough iron in their blood. Many people, mostly children and women, need extra iron. Doctors often suggest that children and

People and animals (left) need oxygen to live. It's easy to spot iron supplements (right) —they're red, just like the color of blood.

women take iron supplements. Of all the vitamins and minerals, iron is the most difficult to get through foods. There are not many foods that are high in iron. The foods highest in iron are meat, poultry, and fish.

Magnesium helps to build strong bones. It also controls your body temperature. Healthy people who eat a variety of foods already get enough magnesium. They don't need to take supple-

Magnesium works with hats, coats, boots, and gloves to keep your body warm in cold weather.

ments. Milk, eggs, cheese, and yogurt contain magnesium. It is also found in meat, seafood, molasses, soybeans, and grain foods (such as oatmeal and cornmeal).

Molasses is a thick syrup that is sometimes poured over pancakes.

Bananas (left) and oranges (right) are excellent sources of potassium.

Potassium is used to make soap. But it is also important because it keeps your heart strong. Potassium also controls how fast your heart beats. Bananas, potatoes, raisins, and melons are just a few of the foods that contain potassium. Other good sources of potassium are oranges, broccoli, and beef.

The salty taste in food comes from sodium. People don't need a lot of sodium to stay healthy. In fact, too much sodium can make a person sick. Doctors suggest that people should not add salt to their food. Enough salt is found in beef, chicken, and vegetables. Most baked

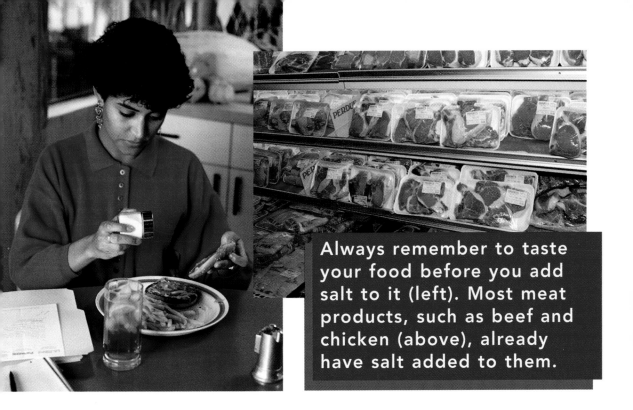

Always remember to taste your food before you add salt to it (left). Most meat products, such as beef and chicken (above), already have salt added to them.

products already have salt added to them.

Zinc is important because it helps your body to heal cuts and scrapes. It also helps your body grow and get stronger. It's important to eat foods that

As you grow, zinc keeps your body strong (above). Grain foods, such as pasta, whole wheat pancakes, cereals, and brown breads (left), all contain the zinc you need for good health.

contain zinc every day. Zinc is found in almost all foods. There is a lot of zinc in oysters, liver, seafood, eggs, peanuts, grain foods, and the dark meat of poultry.

Nutrition Facts

Nutrition labels can be found on cereal boxes and packaged foods. Look for the "Nutrition Facts" on the labels. The facts are a guide for the amounts of vitamins and minerals that you need each day for good health. Nutrition facts help you to choose foods that have the

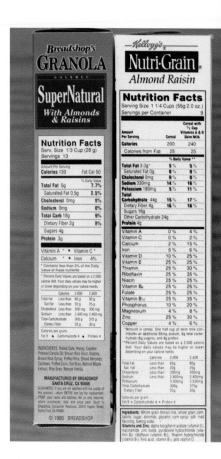

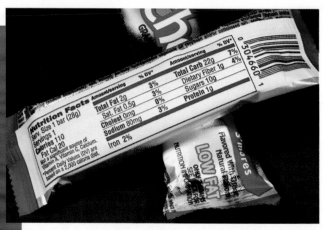

The "Nutrition Facts" on the side panels of some foods (left) list the specific vitamins and minerals that they contain. Most foods, including candy bars (above), have nutrition information on their packaging.

right amounts of important vitamins and minerals.

Eating a variety of healthy foods is the best way to get all the vitamins and minerals you need. And because vita-mins and minerals help every-one to stay healthy, you'll feel good knowing that you're taking care of yourself!

Good health is easy when you eat the right foods.

To Find Out More

Here are some additional resources to help you learn more about vitamins, minerals, and nutrition:

 **Books**

Kalbacken, Joan. **Food Safety.** Children's Press, 1998.

Kalbacken, Joan. **The Food Pyramid.** Children's Press, 1998.

Macmillan Children's Book Staff. **Food.** Knopf, 1997.

Patten, Barbara. **Nutrients: Superstars of Good Health.** Rourke, 1996.

Royston, Angela. **Healthy Me.** Barron, 1995.

Stille, Darlene R. **The Digestive System.** Children's Press, 1997.

Stille, Darlene R. **The Respiratory System.** Children's Press, 1997.

Organizations and Online Sites

National Institutes of Health (NIH)
9000 Rockville Pike
Bethesda, MD 20892
http://www.nih.gov/

A government agency, the NIH works to uncover knowledge that will lead to better health for all Americans. The NIH sponsors research at laboratories, universities, medical schools, and hospitals.

Food and Drug Administration (FDA)
5600 Fishers Lane
Rockville, MD 20857
http://www.fda.gov/

This government agency works to protect the health of the American people by making sure that food is safe, healthy, and clean.

KidsHealth
http://www.kidshealth.org/

Created by medical experts, this site is devoted entirely to the health of children. Contains accurate, up-to-date information about growth, food, fitness, health games, animations, the KidsVote health poll, and lots of surprises!

United States Department of Agriculture (USDA)
14th Street and
  Independence Avenue SW
Washington, DC 20250
*http://www.nal.usda.gov/
fnic/Fpyr/pyramid.html*

This is a group of federal agencies that work to ensure food safety and nutrition, to support American farming, and to conserve our country's natural resources and the environment.

45

Important Words

diet what you eat and drink

growth the way you get taller and bigger

leafy a plant, tree, or vegetable that is covered with leaves

molasses thick, sweet syrup made from sugarcane

operation cutting open a person's body to repair a damaged part or to remove a diseased part

source place where something comes from

substance the important part of something

variety selection of different things

Index

Meet the Author

Joan Kalbacken lives in Normal, Illinois. A former teacher, she taught mathematics and French for twenty-nine years. Ms. Kalbacken is the author of several books for Children's Press, including *Food Safety* and *The Food Pyramid*, companion books to *Vitamins and Minerals.* Ms. Kalbacken is also the recipient of a Distinguished Illinois Author Award from the Illinois Reading Council, and a Merit Teaching Award from the Illinois Those Who Excel Program.